COMPETITIVE
MONOPOLY

The Youth Adventure and Opportunity

ANIK M. SINGH

iUniverse books may be ordered through booksellers or by contacting:

iUniverse
1663 Liberty Drive
Bloomington, IN 47403
www.iuniverse.com
1-800-Authors (1-800-288-4677)

Because of the dynamic nature of the Internet, any web addresses or links contained in this book may have changed since publication and may no longer be valid. The views expressed in this work are solely those of the author and do not necessarily reflect the views of the publisher, and the publisher hereby disclaims any responsibility for them.

Any people depicted in stock imagery provided by Thinkstock are models, and such images are being used for illustrative purposes only.
Certain stock imagery © Thinkstock.

ISBN: 978-1-5320-4235-5 (sc)
ISBN: 978-1-5320-4237-9 (hc)
ISBN: 978-1-5320-4236-2 (e)

Library of Congress Control Number: 2018902010

Print information available on the last page.

iUniverse rev. date: 2/24/2018

CONTENTS

FOREWORD

In March 2012, I was honored to serve as Head Judge for the 5th Annual Grove School MONOPOLY Tournament in Redlands, CA. That's where I first met Anik. At first glance, a scrawny little 4th grader with a winning smile who could barely see over the table where his first-round tournament game was being played would not impress you very much. Cute? Yes. Intimidating to the opposition? No.

But when you consider that this little 4th grader had just traveled over 400 miles with his parents to compete in a charity MONOPOLY tournament against some of the best players in the country, including U.S. & World Championship competitors, then you would have been fairly impressed with his passion, initiative, and vision. Not bad for a little 4th grader with a winning smile.

Anik Looking Overwhelmed at One of his First Youth MONOPOLY Tournaments

Yet when you ALSO witness this little 4th grader firmly stand toe-to-toe (winning smile still intact) against a former U.S. National Championship Finalist in a grueling 90-minute match, while not budging an inch in his negotiation tactics, wheeling & dealing will-power, and beyond-his-years financial prowess, then you would have been dumbfounded. I was.

Anik lost that game, going bankrupt to some unlucky dice. But what impressed me the most was that he kept going. He made the junior division finals later that same day. And he learned his lessons. And four years later, after learning a thousand more life & MONOPOLY lessons, I smiled with great joy when Anik held the trophy (winning smile still very much in place) as the California State MONOPOLY Junior Champion, now a young man capable of spreading fear into the heart of any MONOPOLY player, young or old, with his amazing winning smile, unshakeable sportsmanlike demeanor, incredible drive, and killer will-power, as he makes sure you have the best time in your life laughing along with him while he crushes you with his fine-tuned MONOPOLY prowess (and winning smile)!

As a school teacher myself for over 20 years, I've worked with hundreds of children ages 8 through 18 while using the world's most famous game, MONOPOLY, as an amazing teaching tool to grow children's social, mathematical, and business skills in significant & long-lasting ways. Among those hundreds of young people, Anik is one of the greatest MONOPOLY prodigies I have ever worked with, and his wisdom will deftly guide you through the winning ways of this classic family game.

For MONOPOLY isn't just about "Owning it All"….MONOPOLY teaches life. And Anik will enrich your own life with the wisdom that MONOPOLY has taught him and thousands of others. He has only grown more in the passion, initiative, and vision that I first saw in him more than five years ago. He has since negotiated with multi-million dollar corporations, created large local MONOPOLY clubs, been on local & international TV, and taught countless youth his winning ways. Enjoy your journey with Anik as you Pass GO and collect 200 years' worth of wisdom from an amazing young man!

Tim Vandenberg
2009 U.S. MONOPOLY
National Championship
2nd place

6th Grade Teacher
Hesperia, CA

Instructor
University of Redlands
School of Education

**Mr. Tim Vandenberg and Anik at the
Apple Valley Tournament in 2016.**

DEDICATION

Mr. Harbans Singh (1936-2016)

I want to thank my grandfather, Mr. Harbans Singh, and my family for helping create my passion for business, success, and the competitive spirit.

INTRODUCTION

Few people know the hidden secrets, values, and opportunities of MONOPOLY, a board game we all know and love. My name is Anik Singh, and I would like to personally thank you for choosing to read this book and learn about competitive MONOPOLY. I hope you will learn a lot and that you will share this knowledge and information with your family, friends, and peers so more people can learn about the wonders of competitive MONOPOLY. The values within the game are very important, and I hope you will share them in your community.

Throughout this book, you will learn a little about me, special facts about MONOPOLY, the secrets to competitive success, and what to do with the game in your future. This is a quick, easy-to-read book that is aimed at younger children who are just starting to get into competitive MONOPOLY, though adults may also learn much from it about the most popular board game in the world.

I hope you enjoy reading this book and that it will increase your MONOPOLY expertise. A lot of time, effort, and support have gone into making this project a reality, and I am very honored to write about my experience and to teach other children about the growth and advantages of competitive MONOPOLY. Whether on the game board or in the real world, the information gleaned from the game can help you in many different life situations. I hope you love this book as much as I have loved writing it, and I wish you all the best in your MONOPOLY and life endeavors.

CHAPTER 1

MY MONOPOLY STORY

Anik and his Monopoly Framed Art Collection

You may wonder why I love MONOPOLY, which I've been playing competitively since I was 9 years old. My passion started at the age of 6, when I first encountered MONOPOLY.

Ever since I was a young child, I have always loved the idea of making money. The fact that it gives us so much power to do practically anything in the world makes me really happy. As the youngest of three children, I always dreamt of having some sort of power that would allow me to stand out from my brothers and achieve the most attention, and I realized that winning board games made that possible. I always kept my eyes open for lost coins on the street and thought about what items I could sell for some money.

One day, I stumbled upon my family playing a game of MONOPOLY. They were rolling the dice, exchanging paper money, and trading property between them. Houses and hotels were placed on a square board, along with tokens, and clamor ensued among the players. My heart jumped immediately as I witnessed the action. It didn't take long before I learned how to join the excitement of MONOPOLY, and I did my best whenever I faced any opponent in the household. I wanted to be a successful player, so I tried to adapt new tactics and strategies to show my worth. Because I was only a young child and my family was always busy, I had a lot of free time, and I soon became addicted to the thrill of MONOPOLY, to the point where I felt a strong desire to play it all the time, with anyone who would face me.

Another fun game I put lots of effort into was a video game called *Guitar Hero,* a rock-star simulator in which I had to push color-coded notes on a plastic guitar that matched the notes on the screen. When I couldn't play MONOPOLY with my family, I played *Guitar Hero* alone. Eventually, my childhood consisted almost entirely of *Guitar Hero* and MONOPOLY. I had so much fun with those two games, and I longed to show that I was truly the best at something, to astonish people with my skills and gain the attention I desired.

Once I became a fourth-grader, I noticed that my family really no longer paid any attention to my gaming skills. In other words, my plan didn't work out so well. This frustrated me; not only did I want my family to notice, but I also wanted to show the world that I was good at something. I searched online for *Guitar Hero* tournaments, but unfortunately, the only ones I found were too far away from my home in California, and the minimum age for players was 13. My next-best option was MONOPOLY. Surprisingly, there were local tournaments in Southern California and they only required players to be 8 or older. Best of all, they were held on Saturdays, which meant I wouldn't have to miss school. Jumping with excitement, I asked my parents if I could register, and they agreed. On March 31, 2012, I attended my first MONOPOLY tournament at Grove School in Redlands, California, at the age of 9.

My first tournament experience was one I will forever hold dear to my heart. MONOPOLY tournaments usually consist of two preliminary rounds. Assets gained in those two rounds are added up, and if they are high enough, the player moves on to the final round. All games have a ninety-minute time limit. My first match consisted of four people: two high-schoolers, me, and a very competitive adult, Mr. W. As the game commenced, Mr. W. made some great deals with the high-schoolers, and I could only look on in shock, not sure what to do. Eventually, Mr. W. bankrupted all three of us and made it out with all the money and assets at the end of the ninety minutes. He truly dominated the game. I was speechless and sad and even started to cry.

Shocked and struggling to hold back my tears, I tried harder at the next game and managed to make it out with some assets. Since I knew that there was absolutely no way for me to make the finals at that point, I hesitatingly followed my family to the car. Just as I was bursting into tears, though, as if by magic, my father received a call from the tournament official to inform him that one person had left. Since I had the next-highest amount of assets, I was invited to take that player's spot in the finals. There was a youth final round as well, so I did not have to deal with adults who knew what they were doing. That was a relief, because it felt more fair, as we would all be on an equal playing field when it came to age and experience. My father turned the car around, and we made it back to the tournament in time.

It was a day I will never forget. As I walked in, everyone started clapping for me, and by the end of the round, I had placed fifth in my first youth tournament. Placing in the top five of a competitive event on my rookie run sparked an interest in my heart and created a gleam in my eye. I knew then that I had potential to become competitively strong at that board game. Soon after, I attended more tournaments and learned more about the scene. I even learned more about the game from some MONOPOLY professionals. I placed differently at each tournament, but I learned at every opportunity. In 2016, I managed to win almost all the tournaments I entered, mostly in California towns such as Etiwanda and Apple Valley. My passion for the game wouldn't die down, as I eagerly grabbed every chance to learn more about the game whenever the opportunity presented itself.

Since that first day of competition, I've attended every MONOPOLY tournament I could, and at my new high school, I teach people the secrets I've learned. In all the games I've played, I have come to realize that MONOPOLY is not just a game of luck. It is far more than a roll of the dice. Success in this game involves strategy, persistence, trickery, math, money management, and knowledge. I hope to teach children all over the world not only how to play competitive MONOPOLY but also the benefits of playing.

CHAPTER 2

MISCONCEPTIONS

When most people think about MONOPOLY, the typical thought is that it's a long game that can take many hours to play, that it takes little skill to win, and that, in many ways, it is a colossal waste of time. These are misconceptions, absolutely false. When played correctly, at a maximum of ninety minutes, MONOPOLY forces players to use skill to manipulate the odds of winning, and this involves tricks that differentiate it from other games. A gem of a board game hidden in dusty cupboards, MONOPOLY offers something that not many other games today, old or new, can provide. This game requires social interaction, more so than other famous games. In many games and competitions, a player can win without ever saying a single word to his or her opponents. MONOPOLY, on the other hand, forces players to speak to competitors they may or may not know or have any relationships with, in order to come out with that golden trophy.

If you ask the typical person on the street what they think of MONOPOLY, they will most likely say the game is a huge waste of time, really only a pastime for holiday mornings. The main reason people say this is because most have not learned how to play the right way. Learning the game through experience and social interaction is how people can become knowledgeable about its intricacies. Most people don't know how to play by the actual rules. For example: People place money on Free Parking, which is supposed to be a free spot where nothing happens; some give properties for free to players who roll double-sixes, even though the rules state it only warrants a free roll; and still others invent so-called immunities that allow players to remain safe on property belonging to others, when this is not really legal at all. The list goes on and on. People do not understand how to play MONOPOLY. As a young third-grader, I entered my first tournament without knowing the correct rules, and the result was unfortunate. If people learn to play the game correctly, MONOPOLY will not be a long, drawn-out game, and it will have a far better reputation, the good one it deserves.

"Even if MONOPOLY doesn't have to take that long, it still doesn't take any real skill," many of my friends have told me. I believe they say this because there is no one correct way to play the game. MONOPOLY is so complex that there are many ways to succeed. Thus, the only way to achieve the real strategies of manipulating the odds is by going to tournaments. A search of the Internet will provide many strategies and ways to win, but opinions are divided. Some say Boardwalk and Park Place are the best

TITLE DEED		TITLE DEED	
PARK PLACE		**BOARDWALK**	
Rent	₩35	Rent	₩50
Rent with color set	₩70	Rent with color set	₩100
Rent with 🏠	₩175	Rent with 🏠	₩200
Rent with 🏠🏠	₩500	Rent with 🏠🏠	₩600
Rent with 🏠🏠🏠	₩1100	Rent with 🏠🏠🏠	₩1400
Rent with 🏠🏠🏠🏠	₩1300	Rent with 🏠🏠🏠🏠	₩1700
Rent with 🏨	₩1500	Rent with 🏨	₩2000
Houses cost	₩200 each	Houses cost	₩200 each
Hotels cost	₩200 each (plus 4 houses)	Hotels cost	₩200 each (plus 4 houses)

© 1935, 2017 HASBRO

properties, due to their high value, while others claim the railroads are king due to the probability that they will be landed on. Knowing which properties to trade and trade for, when to mortgage for money, trading negotiations, and token placement are all vital strategies in winning the game. MONOPOLY does involve some luck, yes, but that does not mean it does not also require skill. I will get to these tips and strategies later in this book but for the time being, just realize that MONOPOLY requires a combination and association of skill as well as luck in order to succeed and bankrupt your opponents.

For some reason, many people still think MONOPOLY is a waste of time, and they would rather go do something else. Actually, MONOPOLY provides the perfect combination of thought, strategy, luck, thrill, knowledge, memorization, item placement, probability, social skills, and mind games. In other words, players can enjoy a very exhilarating experience in just an hour or a little longer. Not many other games can do that in such a short amount of time. Also, not many things in this world relate to such a complex board game, but that may unfortunately be part of its downfall. In fact, MONOPOLY is so complex that many people shy away from the game or simply choose not to play it correctly, preferring their own, simpler rules.

All in all, the most common misconceptions of MONOPOLY can be countered, most notably the long amount of time it takes, its supposed lack of skill, and how many better options there are. These are all due to people not really knowing how to play the game by its official rules. MONOPOLY is a quick, entertaining game that can end in ninety minutes, takes intelligence to perform well, and offers some things that no other activity in this generation can compare to. I recommend that you develop a passion for the board game by reading, studying, and learning about MONOPOLY. The skills developed by playing MONOPOLY can be applied to real life and can enhance social skills. Though it may be complex, MONOPOLY is, by far, one of the greatest games for past, current, and future generations.

CHAPTER 3

PRACTICAL MONOPOLY

The Dice

Tournament Play is Exciting

While misconceptions do exist about MONOPOLY, the board game itself offers more than just a fun experience. In a practical sense, it is a game in which players trade with opponents to obtain the upper hand in terms of monetary value and property. What many people don't know is that many skills such as mathematics, manipulation, strategy, and observation define who walks away as the winner. Though the dice may need to be on your side to win from time to time, MONOPOLY incorporates many skills that can be applied to the real world, some of which are even beneficial to children. Learning these skills can lead to real-life success. Success can refer to anything, from winning a competition to doing well in school. Though the differences portray themselves as major, many decisions and actions in life can be related back to the game of MONOPOLY.

Winning a game of MONOPOLY is different from winning any other game. Why? Because rather than finding the correct card deck or perfect reaction time, MONOPOLY requires players to manipulate the odds in their favor. Rolling the dice to see what space you might land on to pay rent, trading with an opponent to obtain a better color group, or making your opponents work to your benefit by giving them a monopoly that isn't as good as yours are just a few examples of manipulating these odds. A trade may appear to be unwise or poor or square even to your opponent, but since you know the positioning, monetary value, and property value, you know you've gotten the better side of the deal. For example, if you give somebody the brown properties (Mediterranean and Baltic Avenues) some of the cheapest and least-likely-to-be-landed-upon properties in the game, while you obtain the orange properties (St. James Place and Tennessee and New York Avenues), among the most frequented spaces on the board, you grant them

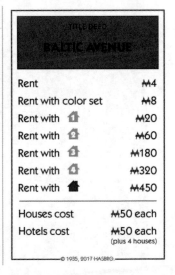

TITLE DEED	
MEDITERRANEAN AVENUE	
Rent	M2
Rent with color set	M4
Rent with 🏠	M10
Rent with 🏠🏠	M30
Rent with 🏠🏠🏠	M90
Rent with 🏠🏠🏠🏠	M160
Rent with 🏨	M250
Houses cost	M50 each
Hotels cost	M50 each (plus 4 houses)
© 1935, 2017 HASBRO	

TITLE DEED	
BALTIC AVENUE	
Rent	M4
Rent with color set	M8
Rent with 🏠	M20
Rent with 🏠🏠	M60
Rent with 🏠🏠🏠	M180
Rent with 🏠🏠🏠🏠	M320
Rent with 🏨	M450
Houses cost	M50 each
Hotels cost	M50 each (plus 4 houses)
© 1935, 2017 HASBRO	

TITLE DEED	TITLE DEED	TITLE DEED
ST. JAMES PLACE	**TENNESSEE AVENUE**	**NEW YORK AVENUE**
Rent Ⓜ14	Rent Ⓜ14	Rent Ⓜ16
Rent with color set Ⓜ28	Rent with color set Ⓜ28	Rent with color set Ⓜ32
Rent with 🏠 Ⓜ70	Rent with 🏠 Ⓜ70	Rent with 🏠 Ⓜ80
Rent with 🏠 Ⓜ200	Rent with 🏠 Ⓜ200	Rent with 🏠 Ⓜ220
Rent with 🏠 Ⓜ550	Rent with 🏠 Ⓜ550	Rent with 🏠 Ⓜ600
Rent with 🏠 Ⓜ750	Rent with 🏠 Ⓜ750	Rent with 🏠 Ⓜ800
Rent with 🏨 Ⓜ950	Rent with 🏨 Ⓜ950	Rent with 🏨 Ⓜ1000
Houses cost Ⓜ100 each	Houses cost Ⓜ100 each	Houses cost Ⓜ100 each
Hotels cost Ⓜ100 each	Hotels cost Ⓜ100 each	Hotels cost Ⓜ100 each
(plus 4 houses)	(plus 4 houses)	(plus 4 houses)
© 1935, 2017 HASBRO	© 1935, 2017 HASBRO	© 1935, 2017 HASBRO

a significantly weaker chance to win the game. Little strategic-thinking moves like that can really turn the tide in a game of MONOPOLY. What might seem simple and not as important can change the whole game. You may be the best player in the world, but nobody can go undefeated in MONOPOLY, as the dice are not always consistent. The game contains elements of success and failure, and the quest is to achieve the maximum amount of wealth possible by bankrupting the other landowners, even while luck dances about from one player to the others. The results of moves in MONOPOLY are similar to the consequences we face in real life. We all want to become the strongest, wealthiest player while also eliminating the competition that lies in front of us. Using methods of manipulation to convince your opponents to make the trade or managing your properties in a special way by mortgaging the weak ones and building houses on the monopoly will take you a long way in the game, just like careful moves and thinking-ahead decisions will take you a long way in life.

Not many games today offer the same satisfaction or experience that MONOPOLY gives. At its best, it is a simple hour-and-a-half game in which a group of four to six people talk, have fun, and enjoy each other. MONOPOLY stands out from the rest with its fast-paced, active game play, the process of trading properties for the benefit of specific players, and the possibility of rolling a seven or eight to go bankrupt on somebody's significantly wealthy property. Things like cell phones and mobile devices, while handy for our human development, do not provide the same benefits as MONOPOLY does. Staring down at a screen isn't the same as actually talking and socializing with friends and family in real life, having a blast while rolling the dice and clutching that paper money in your hand. Though not everybody wants to set up the game or use up two hours of their day, and while some may not enjoy the game as much as others do, the game still holds strong life values that should not be overlooked as we move into the future. All games can be won and lost, but not all carry important life values that you can use in the real world.

CHAPTER 4

SOCIAL SKILLS

Making New MONOPOLY Friends

The board game of MONOPOLY stands out from many other activities, especially in modern culture, because of the necessity of social skills in order to become a great player. In the game, the goal is to bankrupt the rest of your opponents by charging them rent as they land on your property. To increase the rent, you must hold all the colors of a specific color group, the very definition of a monopoly. Once a monopoly is obtained, a player can purchase houses and hotels. Once these are placed, the rent grows exponentially. This is a key point: If you don't own a monopoly (a whole color group) the rent you collect will be very limited, because houses and hotels are necessary to obtain high rent and bankrupt your opponents.

Typically, the properties end up divided between most of the players, limiting the chances to collect high rent. In this case, only one method remains for any player to take ownership of a monopoly: trading, the act of exchanging properties or monetary value between two or more parties. This is where social skills become an essential tool. Without the ability to talk your way into trade, you won't be able to buy color groups and win the game of MONOPOLY. A smart player must be able to communicate nicely and fairly, as no one will trade with a rude or pushy player. Trading involves knowing how to talk your opponents into things, and this is a valuable life skill. Being friendly to your opponents makes you seem like an honest, open person, someone worth doing Business with. Of course, the savvy player can make it all seem like an equal trade, in order to twist the odds of winning, through knowledge of positioning and money obtained. By exchanging properties to achieve your ideal color group, and with a little bit of luck, one can win a game of MONOPOLY solely off social skills in the trading part of the game. Coupled with game knowledge and strategy, these social skills add a significant boost to a player's game play on the board.

Trading properties and gaining a fortune of pastel-colored money through social skills may seem like the only purpose of MONOPOLY, but really, MONOPOLY serves as a stepping stool for real-life social interaction. In today's digital landscape, many people are unable to socially interact on a comfortable level. MONOPOLY can provide that experience, as it is a game that forces players to develop the best social skills to obtain a winning probability against opponents. In one tournament I competed in, I met some new players. In our game, I negotiated a better trade, as I obtained a monopoly while my opponents received cash. As the game went on, their cash slowly decreased and came into my possession, and when the game was over, I was declared the victor. By being polite and pleasant, I managed to persuade a player into doing what I wanted (selling me the monopoly), while also giving my opponent what he wanted (cash). At the end of the day, I won that match with my social skills, and the dice didn't have much to do with that victory at all.

As I was growing up, I was a bit shy about talking to people, as I feared what they would think of me. Then, I noticed my family playing the board game, and I learned more about the game on a competitive level. As I played more competitive MONOPOLY, my social skills grew tremendously. I started talking to adults, teenagers, and other children on a deeper level. The feeling of conquering the art of socialization and becoming a likable, enjoyable person remains one of my favorite sensations. A game that only has forty spaces, seemingly based on luck, is really far more than just a game. MONOPOLY simulates the feelings and social interactions of life itself, all compressed into a small board game. Not many other games today offer that same sense of satisfaction and pleasure. What makes MONOPOLY so special is the diversity of skills that can be applied to real life, all offered within a game that almost everybody can understand, especially social skills. Learning how to control the properties and manipulate the social interactions of the players can significantly help in real-life situations. In the real world, you will endure job interviews, meet new friends, visit unfamiliar places, or have to persuade somebody to let you do something. MONOPOLY will teach you special skills that can help you in all of these situations. Even in our Wi-Fi-connected world, social interaction still impacts our lives no matter where we go. Mastering the skills of talking to others can provide a huge advantage inside and outside of the game.

CHAPTER 5

BUSINESS SKILLS

"At the End of the Day, MONOPOLY is All Business" Anik Singh

Business can be defined as the practice of exchanging goods and services with another partner or partners for the betterment of both parties and their future success. The act of business can be traced back to ancient times, when people exchanged food and materials for survival in unknown lands. It has progressed throughout the years, but we still see business today aiding survival and creating happiness for people around the world. Business is what MONOPOLY is famous for, as one of the key components is the practice of trading properties and money to create monopolies. These monopolies create higher rent for your opponents, making them poorer and you richer. The ability to force your opponents to aid in your success is a skill that is underdeveloped and underrated in the real world, but those who are successful in MONOPOLY know these skills well.

In MONOPOLY, people land on squares that represent properties. They buy these properties with money given to them at the start of the game; everyone starts with the same amount. Once these properties are all bought, the game turns into a strategy game: Whoever can convince his or her opponents to work with them will become the winner. In the previous chapter, I mentioned that being nice can work to your benefit, and this is also true in real life and in business. Nobody would want to work with a rude person in a competitive MONOPOLY game, but if conflicts arise, how can you still initiate a trade your opponent will be happy with? This is where the knowledge and manipulation of the game probabilities can work in your favor.

A typical trade consists of two or more players trading properties, with each player aiming toward owning a monopoly. The trade seems fair, since all the players obtain one monopoly, and all the monopolies seem to be equal. However, some monopolies have a higher probability to be landed on, others have higher rent, and still others can land a quick blow if the players are nearby. Being clear with your communication skills can lead to a victory in the game. Your opponents need to see you as a nice, polite player with great communication skills, someone trying to strike a fair and even deal. In actuality, you must alter the transaction so you get the better end of the deal and have a better chance to win the game.

CHANCE

GO TO JAIL. GO DIRECTLY TO JAIL.
DO NOT PASS GO. DO NOT COLLECT ₥200.

© 1936, 2017 HASBRO.

As an example, let's say Player A wants to own the orange monopoly, because he notices that Player B is in Jail, only a few spaces away from hitting those orange properties. Player B wants the dark blue monopoly, since it is very well known for its return on investment, but Player A is very far away from landing on any dark blue spaces. Player A trades with Player B, and both players end up with the monopoly of their choice. However, since Player A knows his opponent has a greater chance of hitting his monopoly than he does of landing on Player B's spaces, Player A has set himself up for a better chance of winning the game. Luck is still a factor, but landing on a monopoly a few spaces away is better than landing on a monopoly many spaces away. Specific property values and more details are forthcoming in the following chapter.

The whole act of business in MONOPOLY includes more than property values and communication skills. After that monopoly is attained, the next objective is to force opponents to land on your color groups. To move in MONOPOLY, a player rolls two dice and ends up with a number from two to twelve. Remember that the position of your opponents is a key factor in trade. If the opponent is many spaces away, without a clear chance of landing on your monopoly, the chances of getting a hit on your property decrease, also decreasing your chance to win. If the opponent is from six to eighteen spaces away, they will likely have to overcome your monopoly at some point, as there is a great chance they will land on one of your properties. When this happens, they have to pay the rent, and that can be very high, depending on the number of houses or hotels that were built on that specific property. The player who wisely considers the position of the players in proportion to their specific monopoly increases his or her chances of becoming the victor of the game. While you can't really force your opponents to land on your properties, due to slight luck from the dice, you can use the positioning and probability of the dice to determine the chances. Rolling a six, seven, or eight is the most common outcome, while two, three, eleven, or twelve are far less likely.

MONOPOLY gameplay can be divided into three specific stages: growth, business, and outcome. The growth stage pertains to the early part of the game, in which people roll the dice to try to land on and purchase as many properties as possible. The business stage takes place in the middle, when players trade properties to obtain the monopolies they desire. Finally, as its name implies, the outcome stage happens at the end, when players pay rent to others as they land on their monopoly spaces. The business stage is the most important in the game. Without complete knowledge of this stage, it is very difficult to secure a victory in the outcome. Whatever you trade for or with or say about the monopoly you want, can be the breaking point of deciding the winner and loser of a game. If you voice your opinion and manage to make a clear plan of action, you can conquer the business stage, therefore making yourself a stronger MONOPOLY player than ever before.

CHAPTER 6

COMPETITIVE MONOPOLY

Winning is Always Fun!

Competitive MONOPOLY rewards the player who controls the game probability without giving up much wealth. Winners usually maintain friendly relationships in the game, and those players also translate their social skills to real-world settings. Playing actively, being aware of the situations that may lie ahead, and having fundamental knowledge of trade can lead to advantages over your opponents. Though luck does sway things and get in the way of wins from time to time, competitive MONOPOLY requires a different skillset than other games. However, one thing it does share with other games is that specific strategies must be in place during the start, middle, and end of the game to create a greater chance of defeating all the opponents that stand in the way of your golden trophy.

At the start of the game (the growth stage), players roll the dice and attempt to buy every property they land on. These properties later serve as potential trades. The main goal is to obtain bargaining power over your competitors as early as possible. If you are sent to the one space where you are unable to buy any property, Jail, pay to get out as soon as possible. Why? Because properties are just outside those bars, waiting to be obtained! Don't let the opportunity slip away, or your role in the trading part of the game will diminish significantly. Even if you must mortgage your properties to obtain others, do so. Sometimes, the dice get in the way of obtaining many properties. Spaces like Community Chest and Chance do give players money, it is always important to prioritize properties over money, because while money can always be obtained, properties cannot.

There aren't any properties you should specifically avoid, as all are useful at some point. Strategies and plans can make all properties valuable, so never negate the opportunity of obtaining more land. Children, including myself when I was younger, love the sensation of having money, and we think it will protect us in any situation. This mentality hurts many new players and their potential to become competitive MONOPOLY players. Having some money doesn't hurt, but make sure to use it wisely, especially when trying to buy new properties.

Next, the trading stage takes place. It can be argued that this is the most important part of the game, as these few minutes will decide who will win and who will lose the game. Unfortunately, some people won't even take part in it, and their chances of winning decreases. I'll always remember the trading phase of my first MONOPOLY tournament, when I stood as a young child as high-schoolers and adults towered over me, talking about what properties to trade. I let all my opponents obtain properties and build up huge rents, while I sat in my chair clutching my precious money. As time passed, that stack of money dwindled to only a couple dollars. Then, in one final strike, I was bankrupted out of the game. Because I didn't attempt to trade, I unfortunately lost.

There are many ways to trade: trading one on one with properties and money, creating a group of three or four to trade properties, or participating in a mix of all this. All the styles follow the same basic rules of trading. In simple terms, be polite, clear, and open to making a unanimous decision. Most importantly, give them what they want. If your opponents get what they desire, they will be happy with what you obtain. Just be sure to realize if what they want is too aggressive for your liking. If you can convince everybody to obtain what they would like while also getting what you want, you'll make a successful trade.

Certain properties carry better values than others. In MONOPOLY, the value of the property groups increase as you go around the board. Monopolies are color coordinated: brown, light blue, violet, orange, red, yellow, green, and dark blue, as well as railroads and utilities. It's worth knowing the benefits of each of these groups.

The brown properties are too small to make an impact in the late game but can provide some cash you might need to keep you playing. Just don't expect to bankrupt anybody with the brown properties. Only two of them are on the board, so the probability of landing on them is very small.

TITLE DEED MEDITERRANEAN AVENUE	
Rent	M2
Rent with color set	M4
Rent with 🏠	M10
Rent with 🏠🏠	M30
Rent with 🏠🏠🏠	M90
Rent with 🏠🏠🏠🏠	M160
Rent with 🏨	M250
Houses cost	M50 each
Hotels cost	M50 each (plus 4 houses)
© 1935, 2017 HASBRO	

TITLE DEED BALTIC AVENUE	
Rent	M4
Rent with color set	M8
Rent with 🏠	M20
Rent with 🏠🏠	M60
Rent with 🏠🏠🏠	M180
Rent with 🏠🏠🏠🏠	M320
Rent with 🏨	M450
Houses cost	M50 each
Hotels cost	M50 each (plus 4 houses)
© 1935, 2017 HASBRO	

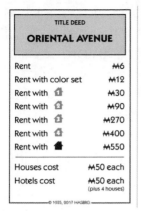

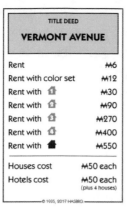

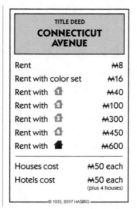

TITLE DEED	
ORIENTAL AVENUE	
Rent	₥6
Rent with color set	₥12
Rent with 🏠	₥30
Rent with 🏠	₥90
Rent with 🏠	₥270
Rent with 🏠	₥400
Rent with 🏨	₥550
Houses cost	₥50 each
Hotels cost	₥50 each (plus 4 houses)

© 1935, 2017 HASBRO

TITLE DEED	
VERMONT AVENUE	
Rent	₥6
Rent with color set	₥12
Rent with 🏠	₥30
Rent with 🏠	₥90
Rent with 🏠	₥270
Rent with 🏠	₥400
Rent with 🏨	₥550
Houses cost	₥50 each
Hotels cost	₥50 each (plus 4 houses)

© 1935, 2017 HASBRO

TITLE DEED	
CONNECTICUT AVENUE	
Rent	₥8
Rent with color set	₥16
Rent with 🏠	₥40
Rent with 🏠	₥100
Rent with 🏠	₥300
Rent with 🏠	₥450
Rent with 🏨	₥600
Houses cost	₥50 each
Hotels cost	₥50 each (plus 4 houses)

© 1935, 2017 HASBRO

The light blue monopoly offers moderate cash. The properties are cheap, but in this case, you get what you pay for, because they are inferior to the more expensive ones. These are great for cash flow and can bankrupt other players, but they are easily outclassed. It's best to use these earlier in the game, rather than later. When it comes to high rents, the light blues are unable to keep up with the competition.

The violet properties are really the most average. These properties are a great return on investment, are somewhat cheap, and are located in a corner of the board near Jail. They can win games with a little luck on your side. Hotels are necessary for violets, averaging at around $750 per hit.

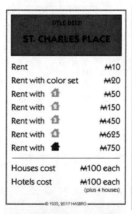

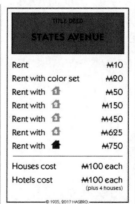

TITLE DEED	
ST. CHARLES PLACE	
Rent	₥10
Rent with color set	₥20
Rent with 🏠	₥50
Rent with 🏠	₥150
Rent with 🏠	₥450
Rent with 🏠	₥625
Rent with 🏨	₥750
Houses cost	₥100 each
Hotels cost	₥100 each (plus 4 houses)

© 1935, 2017 HASBRO

TITLE DEED	
STATES AVENUE	
Rent	₥10
Rent with color set	₥20
Rent with 🏠	₥50
Rent with 🏠	₥150
Rent with 🏠	₥450
Rent with 🏠	₥625
Rent with 🏨	₥750
Houses cost	₥100 each
Hotels cost	₥100 each (plus 4 houses)

© 1935, 2017 HASBRO

TITLE DEED	
VIRGINIA AVENUE	
Rent	₥12
Rent with color set	₥24
Rent with 🏠	₥60
Rent with 🏠	₥180
Rent with 🏠	₥500
Rent with 🏠	₥700
Rent with 🏨	₥900
Houses cost	₥100 each
Hotels cost	₥100 each (plus 4 houses)

© 1935, 2017 HASBRO

TITLE DEED	
ST. JAMES PLACE	
Rent	₥14
Rent with color set	₥28
Rent with 🏠	₥70
Rent with 🏠	₥200
Rent with 🏠	₥550
Rent with 🏠	₥750
Rent with 🏨	₥930
Houses cost	₥100 each
Hotels cost	₥100 each (plus 4 houses)

© 1935, 2017 HASBRO

TITLE DEED	
TENNESSEE AVENUE	
Rent	₥14
Rent with color set	₥28
Rent with 🏠	₥70
Rent with 🏠	₥200
Rent with 🏠	₥550
Rent with 🏠	₥750
Rent with 🏨	₥950
Houses cost	₥100 each
Hotels cost	₥100 each (plus 4 houses)

© 1935, 2017 HASBRO

TITLE DEED	
NEW YORK AVENUE	
Rent	₥16
Rent with color set	₥32
Rent with 🏠	₥80
Rent with 🏠	₥220
Rent with 🏠	₥600
Rent with 🏠	₥800
Rent with 🏨	₥1000
Houses cost	₥100 each
Hotels cost	₥100 each (plus 4 houses)

© 1935, 2017 HASBRO

The orange properties are known to be the best in the game. They are in the perfect spot, away from the most landed-on space in the board (Jail), they are cheap to build on, and they can make an impact in the late game. These should be the properties you aim to obtain.

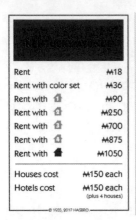

KENTUCKY AVENUE

Rent	₼18
Rent with color set	₼36
Rent with 🏠	₼90
Rent with 🏠	₼250
Rent with 🏠	₼700
Rent with 🏠	₼875
Rent with 🏨	₼1050
Houses cost	₼150 each
Hotels cost	₼150 each (plus 4 houses)

© 1935, 2017 HASBRO

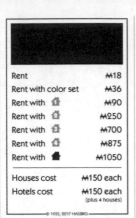

INDIANA AVENUE

Rent	₼18
Rent with color set	₼36
Rent with 🏠	₼90
Rent with 🏠	₼250
Rent with 🏠	₼700
Rent with 🏠	₼875
Rent with 🏨	₼1050
Houses cost	₼150 each
Hotels cost	₼150 each (plus 4 houses)

© 1935, 2017 HASBRO

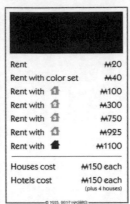

ILLINOIS AVENUE

Rent	₼20
Rent with color set	₼40
Rent with 🏠	₼100
Rent with 🏠	₼300
Rent with 🏠	₼750
Rent with 🏠	₼925
Rent with 🏨	₼1100
Houses cost	₼150 each
Hotels cost	₼150 each (plus 4 houses)

© 1935, 2017 HASBRO

The red monopoly stands out as expensive but provides lots of cash and has a high probability of being landed on. Red is widely considered to be the second-best color group, and it is best to purchase or trade for these if you cannot obtain the oranges.

The yellows are almost identical to the reds, as they earn more rent but are less likely to be landed on. The MONOPOLY community generally sees them in similar regard to the violets, and they are great in almost every aspect, but nothing stands out for them.

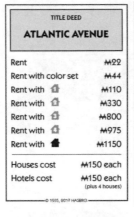

TITLE DEED

ATLANTIC AVENUE

Rent	₼22
Rent with color set	₼44
Rent with 🏠	₼110
Rent with 🏠	₼330
Rent with 🏠	₼800
Rent with 🏠	₼975
Rent with 🏨	₼1150
Houses cost	₼150 each
Hotels cost	₼150 each (plus 4 houses)

© 1935, 2017 HASBRO

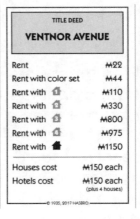

TITLE DEED

VENTNOR AVENUE

Rent	₼22
Rent with color set	₼44
Rent with 🏠	₼110
Rent with 🏠	₼330
Rent with 🏠	₼800
Rent with 🏠	₼975
Rent with 🏨	₼1150
Houses cost	₼150 each
Hotels cost	₼150 each (plus 4 houses)

© 1935, 2017 HASBRO

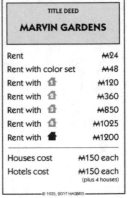

TITLE DEED

MARVIN GARDENS

Rent	₼24
Rent with color set	₼48
Rent with 🏠	₼120
Rent with 🏠	₼360
Rent with 🏠	₼850
Rent with 🏠	₼1025
Rent with 🏨	₼1200
Houses cost	₼150 each
Hotels cost	₼150 each (plus 4 houses)

© 1935, 2017 HASBRO

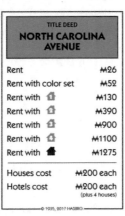

TITLE DEED

PACIFIC AVENUE

Rent	₼26
Rent with color set	₼52
Rent with 🏠	₼130
Rent with 🏠	₼390
Rent with 🏠	₼900
Rent with 🏠	₼1100
Rent with 🏨	₼1275
Houses cost	₼200 each
Hotels cost	₼200 each (plus 4 houses)

© 1935, 2017 HASBRO

TITLE DEED

NORTH CAROLINA AVENUE

Rent	₼26
Rent with color set	₼52
Rent with 🏠	₼130
Rent with 🏠	₼390
Rent with 🏠	₼900
Rent with 🏠	₼1100
Rent with 🏨	₼1275
Houses cost	₼200 each
Hotels cost	₼200 each (plus 4 houses)

© 1935, 2017 HASBRO

TITLE DEED

PENNSYLVANIA AVENUE

Rent	₼28
Rent with color set	₼56
Rent with 🏠	₼150
Rent with 🏠	₼450
Rent with 🏠	₼1000
Rent with 🏠	₼1200
Rent with 🏨	₼1400
Houses cost	₼200 each
Hotels cost	₼200 each (plus 4 houses)

© 1935, 2017 HASBRO

The greens may seem great at first, but the group is not that lucrative. On green, houses and hotels are hard to build, and rarely do players land on these spaces. Honestly, green is nearly as bad as browns or light blues, though the green monopoly has high rent, if you have enough money to spend on it.

The dark blue properties are the MONOPOLY wildcard. These two properties charge the highest rent in the game and are the hardest to build. However, if an opponent is unfortunate enough to land on one, the rent will surely be enough to knock them out or cripple them significantly.

TITLE DEED	
PARK PLACE	
Rent	₩35
Rent with color set	₩70
Rent with 🏠	₩175
Rent with 🏠🏠	₩500
Rent with 🏠🏠🏠	₩1100
Rent with 🏠🏠🏠🏠	₩1300
Rent with 🏨	₩1500
Houses cost	₩200 each
Hotels cost	₩200 each
	(plus 4 houses)

© 1935, 2017 HASBRO

TITLE DEED	
BOARDWALK	
Rent	₩50
Rent with color set	₩100
Rent with 🏠	₩200
Rent with 🏠🏠	₩600
Rent with 🏠🏠🏠	₩1400
Rent with 🏠🏠🏠🏠	₩1700
Rent with 🏨	₩2000
Houses cost	₩200 each
Hotels cost	₩200 each
	(plus 4 houses)

© 1935, 2017 HASBRO

READING RAILROAD

RENT	₩25
If 2 Railroads are owned	₩50
If 3 Railroads are owned	₩100
If 4 Railroads are owned	₩200

© 1935, 2017 HASBRO

PENNSYLVANIA RAILROAD

RENT	₩25
If 2 Railroads are owned	₩50
If 3 Railroads are owned	₩100
If 4 Railroads are owned	₩200

© 1935, 2017 HASBRO

B. & O. RAILROAD

RENT	₩25
If 2 Railroads are owned	₩50
If 3 Railroads are owned	₩100
If 4 Railroads are owned	₩200

© 1935, 2017 HASBRO

SHORT LINE

RENT	₩25
If 2 Railroads are owned	₩50
If 3 Railroads are owned	₩100
If 4 Railroads are owned	₩200

© 1935, 2017 HASBRO

ELECTRIC COMPANY

If one Utility is owned, rent is 4 times amount shown on dice.

If both Utilities are owned, rent is 10 times amount shown on dice.

© 1935, 2017 HASBRO

WATER WORKS

If one Utility is owned, rent is 4 times amount shown on dice.

If both Utilities are owned, rent is 10 times amount shown on dice.

© 1935, 2017 HASBRO

The railroads can obtain a maximum of $200 a hit if you own all four of them. They mainly serve as a supplement for building houses on a monopoly you own. Similar to the railroads, the main use of the utilities is extra revenue, and they max out at $120. These monopolies should not be used to deal damage; rather, they will help you raise money for the houses you want to build.

Just because some monopolies are better than others does not mean you should limit yourself to one or a few color groups. You might not have enough money to build up on that monopoly, so it's good to have a monopoly that is easier to build on. It is also smart to take the position of your opponents into account. If your opponents are six to eighteen spaces away, that monopoly—no matter its color—can allow you to obtain rent quickly. If opponents are more than twenty-five spaces away, it's going to be some time before you can collect from them.

BOARDWALK

MORTGAGE
VALUE ₼200

TO UNMORTGAGE,
PAY ₼220

Card must be turned this side up
if property is mortgaged.

PARK PLACE

MORTGAGE
VALUE ₼175

TO UNMORTGAGE,
PAY ₼193

Card must be turned this side up
if property is mortgaged.

In the outcome stage of the game, based on your decisions in the trading phase, players come out owning various color groups. Once you have obtained yours, mortgage all the properties that are not doing anything significant. If a property is making only ten dollars per hit, for instance, it is best to mortgage that property and cash in on its value. If you mortgage a property, when somebody lands on it, no revenue will be gained. Though this may seem like a downside, the money you obtain from mortgaging is immediate, making this an excellent strategy to obtain your houses as soon as the color group is within your possession. Then, combined with your money, build up as many houses as you can. The best strategy is to build to the three-house level on every single property, as the money per hit goes up significantly. After you have your houses, if luck and probability go your way, you will come out victorious. As the bankruptcies occur, the rich get richer, and the poor get poorer.

Competitive MONOPOLY is unique because it follows a different formula than what we usually see today. With the growth, trading, and outcome stages leading the way, MONOPOLY offers an amazing experience that truly feels like a joyful ride. Though the game is competitive, at the end of the day, MONOPOLY is a cheerful, enjoyable, educational experience with friends or family, and that joy is sustained in such a strategic game, no matter how many times you play.

CHAPTER 7

TOURNAMENTS

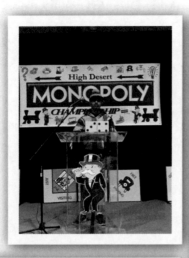

Go Global with MONOPOLY!

MONOPOLY tournaments are the ultimate way to test your game skills. These take place around the world. To find one, look for MONOPOLY tournament websites. Tournament play is different from playing at home or against your friends, since you will compete with strangers you don't know, in an unknown environment, many of whom speak different languages and use different styles and strategies of play. You will build friendships with people you've never met before. Through tournaments, not only will you find more competition and opportunities to show your skills, but you will also gain more insight about yourself as a person. These insights can be anything from how to treat people to differences that can be made to your playing style. Once you decide to take the next step in your MONOPOLY journey, it is time to travel to tournaments to see how you fare against the rest of the community.

Please make sure you read the rules of the tournament before going, as MONOPOLY tournaments differ from event to event. Typically, though, all tournaments follow a similar format:

- Opening announcements
- Two to three preliminary rounds
- Lunch
- A semifinal round
- A final round
- Awards ceremony

Based on the first two rounds, the tournament director uses a system to award points, and players move through the tournament to the semifinals and finals. Whoever wins the semifinal tables advances to the finals, and the winner of the finals is considered the champion. As I've mentioned, each game takes about ninety minutes, along with a lunch break after the second round, with some breaks between rounds. Tournaments typically start at eight a.m. and end at four p.m.

If possible, try to register for local tournaments. Not only does playing well in the tournament matter, but meeting new friends and knowing your local tournament scene can go a long way to becoming great at the game. MONOPOLY tournaments offer an experience of friendly, open competition and fun times outside the games. The world of tournaments opens up the endless possibilities of MONOPOLY. It will better your game skills, improve your social and business skills, and help you learn how to strategically take on tasks and responsibilities in the real world.

Once you have entered a few tournaments, you may even want to try creating your own. This might seem like a large jump, but hosting a tournament is rather easy. Establishing the tournament scene for your specific region creates a special community in which people can play MONOPOLY with an incentive to become the best, and all will look forward to lots of fun. Not only that, but MONOPOLY tournaments can also generate profit based on the number of entrants, and you can donate that money to charity, schools, or special organizations. The best part is that creating a competitive tournament environment does not require too much of an investment or too many resources. All you need are a few tables, MONOPOLY boards, players, and a method to keep score. The more tournaments there are around the world, the greater the passion for the great game of MONOPOLY will be.

MONOPOLY tournaments will allow you to give real money to places that need it! Invigorate the competitive MONOPOLY scene to reach new heights for the betterment of the community. Caring for others goes a long way, even in the spirit of competitive MONOPOLY. Though MONOPOLY is typically known as a game to be played with family and friends, organizing tournaments and generating local interest in MONOPOLY offers more benefits than most people realize.

I have had the personal pleasure of organizing many tournaments. My favorite was the California State Championship at the largest permanent MONOPOLY board in the world in downtown San Jose in 2016. It was a great event, and I look forward to more like it in my community.

Anik Resting on the Largest Permanent MONOPOLY Board in San Jose, CA

CHAPTER 8

MONOPOLY AND YOUR FUTURE

Anik Visiting Hasbro Headquarters in Providence, Rhode Island

Competitive MONOPOLY specializes in enhancing your game skills and helping you communicate better with people even outside the game. Tournaments are a good start, but there are many more opportunities to apply those MONOPOLY lessons that will help you grow as an individual. I like using MONOPOLY to enhance my passion for community service and philanthropy. Typically, the goal in MONOPOLY is to bankrupt all your opponents and become the wealthiest businessperson. Out in the real world, standing out from the crowd and shaping a successful future for yourself is important, but your real goal should be to benefit others by using skills that are attainable from competitive MONOPOLY.

Though this may seem drastically different from the game plan we all know from MONOPOLY, you can use the MONOPOLY foundation in everyday life. How is this possible? In the previous chapter, I mentioned tournaments as a starting point for learning more about the game. This still stands true, and it will help you instruct young players as you learn more about the competitive nature and strategies of the game by entering local tournaments and meeting intelligent opponents. In my first tournament, I was bankrupted quite quickly, but after that, MONOPOLY experts tutored me and taught me much about the game. By participating in tournaments, you will learn more about competitive MONOPOLY as a whole and learn how to play the game at a competitive level. You will also learn skills that you can apply to social and business situations. Getting young players into tournaments is the first step toward increasing understanding of the game, and, therefore, how to use those MONOPOLY learnings in real-life situations.

In addition to tournaments, MONOPOLY is a great opportunity for community service. Taking some time out of your day to teach others about real-life skills and strategies gleaned from the game can make everyone feel happier. People can learn more, beyond what is typically taught. I recommend that all MONOPOLY fans teach other children MONOPOLY as a method to develop their social and business understanding, thereby making them more successful. Teaching others these skills enables them to make friends, keep conversations going, trade and bargain effectively, and much more. Little acts of kindness to spread awareness about the game and the skill set that accompanies MONOPOLY certainly increase social, math, business, and quantitative skills out in the real world. People need help, and through MONOPOLY, you can give others the skills of better judgment and communication and strategic thinking, all of which will come in handy in real life.

Philanthropy, also known as charity, is really important to communities, and raising money for various worthy causes is a great way to help others. By hosting fundraising MONOPOLY tournaments and events, we can create a better place for others. It could be argued that philanthropy successfully combines the benefits of community service and tournaments, and the best part is that we can give back to the community that needs the support the most. Philanthropy serves as a bridge to entertain individuals who don't use or know about competitive MONOPOLY and encourages the people who do know about competitive MONOPOLY to spread their joy and passion for the game with help for others. More opportunities and chances to grow the scene even more also stem from philanthropy, as a little bonus for the generosity provided.

MONOPOLY, at its core, is a game that attracts many people. What many don't know about is the competitive factor, which increases skills and intelligence that can be practically applied in the real world. When we take advantage of tournament and event opportunities, community service, and philanthropy, the game grows, and we help others. As we teach more people, not only do we grow interest in MONOPOLY, but we also change our futures for the betterment of society.

CHAPTER 9

CONCLUSIONS

Anik at his Favorite Tournament (Apple Valley, California, 2015)

Congratulations on reading all the way to the end of this book! I hope you have enjoyed it as much as I enjoyed writing it, as I am always thrilled when more children discover the exciting world of MONOPOLY that I have experienced. I also hope you will get out there and invite others to join the MONOPOLY community.

MONOPOLY is a game that carries so many important values, things our society seems to have lost or is missing. The social skills that can be acquired from MONOPOLY can take people very far. The applicable business skills can be of service as well, since money is all around us and is used every day. Becoming adept at the game of MONOPOLY will not only make you successful on the board but also provides the long-term benefits of social, business, math, and strategy skills in the real world. When the time arises to use these skills, you will be ready to tackle those challenges head on.

MONOPOLY has been one of my passions for a long time, and it is still one of my favorite things to do. The game offers so much that is hidden from the naked eye. Growing the community by hosting a tournament and helping charities and people in need with the money from them is as exciting as the MONOPOLY scene itself. By cultivating this awareness and accessibility of the game, we can help our communities become places where people are comfortable using skills that are vital in the real world. I thank you very much for your kindness in reading this book, and I hope you continue your MONOPOLY career.

ABOUT THE AUTHOR

Anik M. Singh is 15 years old. He was born in Stanford, California and presently lives in Los Altos Hills, California. He is the youngest of three children and has two older brothers to look up to. Anik is presently a high school student at Bellarmine College Preparatory in San Jose, California, where he serves as President and Founder of Club Bellopoly, an after-school MONOPOLY club that raises money for important causes and community service as educators. Anik has been involved in competitive MONOPOLY in California as a player, promoter, and tournament organizer. He is a ranked California youth MONOPOLY champion, a Junior Board Member with the Friends of San Jose (MONOPOLY in the Park), and served as Hasbro's Youth Ambassador for the 2015 World MONOPOLY Championship in Macau, Hong Kong. Anik looks forward to studying economics in college when he finishes high school. His favorite MONOPOLY token is the classic race car.

Club Bellopoly at Bellarmine College Preparatory

ACKNOWLEDGMENTS

Anik with Mr. Lee Bayrd: First Monopoly World Champion

I would like to personally thank the many people who have helped me in my MONOPOLY journey. I have been fortunate to have made many friends in the American MONOPOLY circuit. Many have become my mentors and supporters, including Mr. Lee Bayrd, Mr. Ken Koury, and Mr. Kevin Tostado. I also want to thank all the members of the California MONOPOLY circuit who have shared their skills with me. I want to especially thank Mr. Timothy Vandenberg for his education, passion, and continued support of my MONOPOLY career since my younger days. He has truly been a role model and is the mentor I admire the most. I would also like to recognize and thank Ms. Ashley Fedor for her help with manuscript organization and review.

Living near San Jose, California, I have been very blessed to have the largest MONOPOLY board in the world in my community. I want to thank Mrs. Jill Cody and Mr. Jose Posadas for allowing me to be a strategist and advisor to the Friends of San Jose as they manage MONOPOLY in the Park. It gives me great excitement to know that my Club Bellopoly continues to teach the future leaders of the game. I want

Anik with Ms. Jill Cody

Anik Recruiting for Club Bellopoly

to thank Mr. Chris Meyercord and Father Mario Prietto for allowing me to continue my MONOPOLY growth and allowing our club the resources to succeed.

In addition, I want to thank the MONOPOLY leadership team at Hasbro in Rhode Island for allowing me to develop further as a MONOPOLY enthusiast. Personal thanks to Mr. Adam Kleinman for the opportunity to experience the highest level of MONOPOLY at the World Championship in Macau in September of 2015. A big thanks to Mr. Vadim Denishenko and the Hasbro marketing team for their unwavering support of this book with their approval.

Anik with Team Hasbro in August 2017

Finally, none of this would be possible without my family. I thank my parents for their dedication and for encouraging my passion, for helping me follow my MONOPOLY dreams. I am grateful to my two brothers for always challenging me to be the best I can, in all phases of life.

Anik and his Winning Ways!

GOOD LUCK!

Printed in the United States
By Bookmasters